Homecare

How to start a new home healthcare business in the United States...

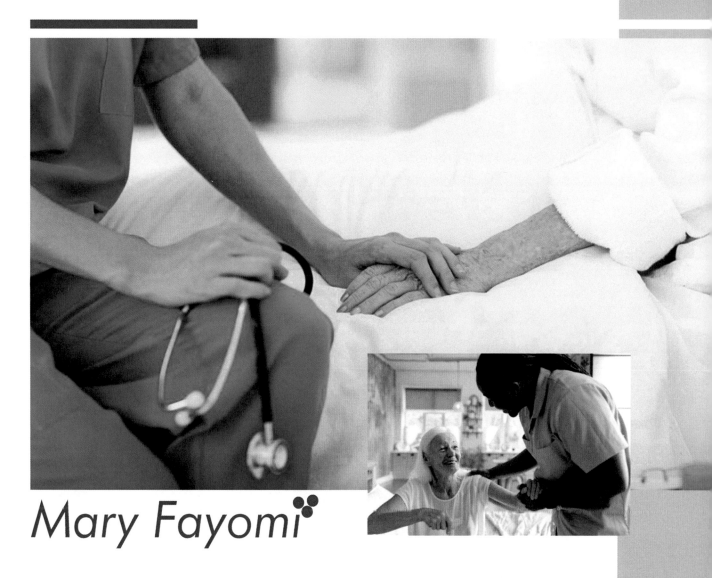

Mary Fayomi

Homecare

How to start a new home healthcare business in the United States...

COPYRIGHT @ 2023 BY MARY FAYOMI
ISBN: 9798372853010

Published By:

Vision Power Publishers

P. O Box 2611,

Arlington TX. 76004
www.visionpowerpublishers.com

CONTENTS

Dedication

DEDICATED TO MY GRANDCHILDREN

Introduction

Home health care consist of a wide range of professional health services rendered to individual patients by healthcare professionals in conjunction with a physician's order at the client's home. Home health care business services include both medical care that is provided by skilled nurses (i.e physical therapy, occupational therapy, Medical social services and respiratory therapy), while non-medical or traditional home health care consist of only personal care support.

1

However, patients may apply for any of the home healthcare services and pay for out of pocket. Usually, many people would qualify for services through, Medicare, Medicaid and private insurance due to age and disability.

Every state in the United States has its own specific instructions for application, amount of fee payment, time requirement, rules and regulations. This book is based on my own experience as a retired owner of home health care organization. A home health care agency is easier to start today than previously because of many consulting opportunities such as virtual service providers and franchise agencies that would start a legitimate and stress-free home health care business in a timely manner, if you can afford the start-up cost.

This book would provide information about the option of "doing it yourself" based on my personal experience and achievements. Although, it may require more time, commitments, and energy but the benefits may include, but not limited to: less start-up funds, better understanding of the foundational knowledge of how to be the CEO of your own business.

People may be asking question about who can have home care business. The response will be "Anyone" can be the owner of home healthcare agency in as much as the candidate is ready to comply with rules and regulations of the state's health department. There are basically 4 phases in the process of starting new home healthcare business: the brainstorming, preparation for the business, providing the services and exiting the business.

the Brainstorming Phase

This phase involves you deciding if starting a home health agency is for you. The following few questions would also be helpful:

- Do you Know yourself and what you are capable of?
- What is the type of home healthcare service(s) that you would like to provide ?
- Do you have the inspiration to run your own business?
- What is your vision?
- Are you confident in your abilities to run this business?
- How much start-up funds do you have for the business?

5

▪ Do you have a vested interest in the care of the patients you will be servicing or are you in it for the money?

▪ Can you listen attentively and solve problems?

▪ Can you read, write and navigate electronics devices (i.e. technology savvy)?

▪ Do you have a reliable mode of transportation?

▪ Are you very healthy and energetic?

Then take a deep breath about your answers and pray for good luck.

Many people would say that it is easy to operate home health agency; some would say it is difficult, while others would just keep quiet without sharing their opinion. The opinion of people about home health care business are different. Sometimes, the resources of funds may be low due to less case load, inadequate staffing no matter how much, frequent training requirements for your employee(s). If the employee(s) is not committed, other providers may take your client.

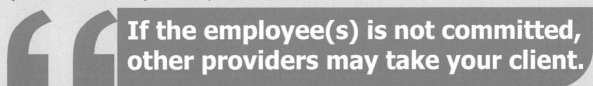

If the employee(s) is not committed, other providers may take your client.

State inspectors may issue violations during an audit with big recoupment, many unanswered calls from Medicare, Medicaid, the State, Private health Insurance, Physician's office, handling the usual issues of difficult clients and their families.

7

Generally, the experience of each day is different and unique as it relates to the management of a home health care business; hence, all those questions/qualities in the previous paragraph are required to help function and cope with good and bad days. However, the 5-Ws of HIPPA (The health insurance Portability and Accountability Act of 1996) Such as WHO, WHY, WHEN, WHERE, and HOW are good tools to use when starting a home health care business.

The Preparation Phase

The preparation phase is the actual acceptance of digging yourself into the business, getting ready to build the foundation for the business and using the services of other experts to achieve your goal. For example, an accounting officer would be needed to perform 'financial forecast for the first year since the business may not generate adequate funds within the first year of providing services.

The next step is to Search and get a name for the business. Then, contact the IRS to obtain a Tax ID and EIN numbers. Then, obtain and complete application form on department of health website.

The form would require certain information like the name and demographic information of the applicant, description of the services to be provided and the start date. When the application has been approved, the State would mandate the policy and procedure for the services which is the reference materials of the provider .

 The State may require a proficiency examination by a Certified Nurse Assistant (CNA) to do the mandatory proficiency state test.

10

The policy and procedure is like a dictionary that guides the services therefore, it requires full review and understanding. The State may require a proficiency examination by a Certified Nurse Assistant (CNA) to do the mandatory proficiency state test. At this point, the business telephone, and fax numbers should have been obtained. A business bank account should be opened and contain the deposit of the required amount of funds by the State department of health. Since the process may be different in each state, people must get information at the State in which the business would be performed.

Office Space

❀

The office space can be set up either in your home or rented office space. Set up the office according to your business need and get the following office supplies: Laptop, printer, stationery, medical supply and daily utilities. The business must have a website, logo, letterhead, flyer for advertising, business cards, photo camera for passport photo of employee and the machine to upload job ID.

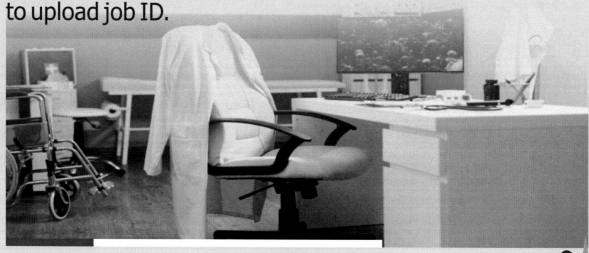

Hiring of Employee(s)

The agency must design a legal employment package according to State requirements before the start of employment. The First staff hires should include yourself as CEO or director of nursing if you a registered nurse, RN/ Quality Assurance (QA) or CNA, and an office secretary.

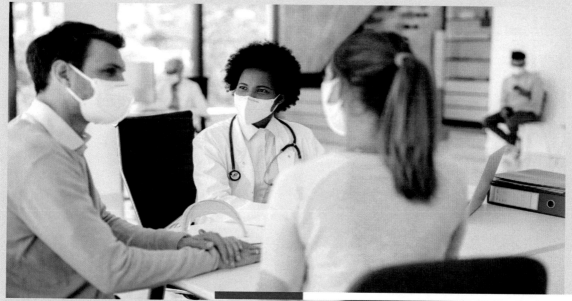

13

Apart from admission of patients and training of nursing staff, the RN/QA would be responsible for reviewing/ obtaining the required functioning documents listed below:

- Reviewing information of Medicare, Medicaid, CMS, CDC and private health Insurance
- Developing the policy and procedure document for your Agency
- The tax employment status
- How to get business liability Insurance
- The medical bags for visiting nurse
- The list for medical supplies

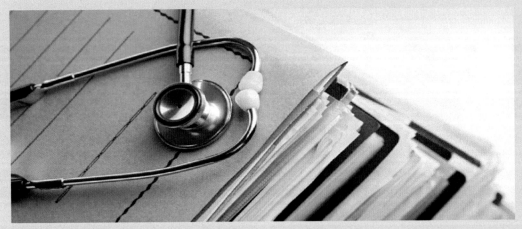

- The list for Wound care and intravenous fluids
- The Employee folder
- The patient's folder
- The skill forms folder
- The Quality Assurance folder
- The Incident and accident folder
- The employee training folder
- The Patient home folder
- The Drug free workplace folder
- The Professional License verification folder
- The Employment benefits folder
- The Scheduling folder
- The Criminal background folder
- The Immunization folder
- The Worker's compensation folder
- The Immigration Folder
- The State's survey folder
- The Agency communication folder

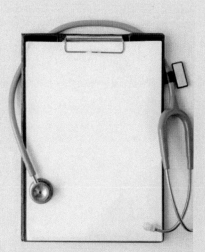

The Service Providing Phase

Start well, continue to do well, and follow up to do well. The next step is to advertise the business to targeted clientele in relevant local newspaper, flyers/business cards, visit religious organizations to discuss your business services and visit medical offices within your community to talk about the services.

16

For the State to set up the first survey and issue a temporary license, the agency must have been providing services to at least 2 clients. I would encourage new business owners to provide voluntary home healthcare services for about 2 patients for at least 6 weeks while getting ready for the state survey.

Prior to calling the State for the initial survey, it is very paramount to conduct a mock survey by the RN/QA who would make sure that those 2 clients are getting services according to the Physician order, plan of care and State regulations. When the agency makes the call to the State department of community health for the readiness of the survey, the State surveyor would schedule the appointment to review the folders of the agency and conduct home visit of the 2 clients to confirm the accuracy of the clinical services to the clients.

> **I would encourage new business owners to provide voluntary home healthcare services for about 2 patients for at least 6 weeks.**

If the surveyor has been satisfied with ZERO violation, the NPI (National provider Identification) number and initial practicing license would then be issued for the agency.

The agency would be encouraged to keep up the same quality of services according to the regulations and plan of care of their clients, so that future survey could yield positive results and to prevent violation and recoupment at each survey. Subsequent State surveys may not require an appointment, as it depends on the objective for the survey. There are many types of surveys such as normal or regular survey which are conducted within the calendar. The survey may be based on complaints from clients or

18

caregiver hence the agency must do the right thing all the time.

The State would continue to send clients to the agency according to Policy. It is the responsibility of the agency to perform marketing ads for private clients and register with non-Government healthcare Insurance company and attend meetings of community health services. Although, it is not the responsibility of the State to provide clients for the agency, sometimes the rotational policy for client assignment may not get to your agency frequency. This is why the regulations of the State may mandate home healthcare agency accept all assigned clients unless the service would be unsafe for the client. No provider may reject the assignment of clients.

When the caseload increases, the staffing should increase. Even if the agency has only 2 clients, the State regulation would treat your agency like others that carries 50 caseloads; therefore, you will be surveyed every 8 months or randomly depends on what the State requirements are. The State has the power to monitor and close the agency for illegal and fraudulent activities.

The Exit Stage

While the exit plan for any business may seem simple and straightforward, exiting a home healthcare business requires additional documentations and specific procedures to close the business. The exit stage may happen earlier than expected due to changes in the environment such as Aging/health condition of the owner, financial hardship,

retirement, relocation, etc which can lead to the options of either selling or dissolving the business. The exit phase is more complicated than the starting phase of a home health care business, but the section of this book will provide in-depth information about the exit plan in a clean way.

There are various ways to exit from home care agency such as business dissolution, selling the business and franchising the business. The procedure to release the business to a buyer or franchise is different from dissolution of the business, which is the point being addressed below.

The procedure of dissolution of the business are as follows:

1.   Obtain and complete the form for the intent to terminate the business from the office of the Secretary of State Corporations Division.

2. Submit the letter of intent to dissolve and exit from the business at least 4 weeks before dissolution. The letter must include last day to cease accepting clients, the transfer of current caseloads to another active home healthcare agency. The State would then schedule appointment for a final state survey.

3. The final state survey would be conducted. The letter of business dissolution would be issued if the agency achieves a successful result of Zero violation.

4. **patient and employment records** must be maintained for **6 years** after dissolution of the business. After the dissolution of the business according to the regulations of the State, these items must be in the custody of the CEO, well preserved and protected for **6 years** following dissolution.

5. Make payment for any outstanding bills.

23

6. Send the letter of business dissolution to the following organization:

- The state County
- The Workers compensation
- The business liability Insurance
- The Department of labor.
- Medicare and Medicaid office
- The office of private Insurance
- The IRS
- The website domain company
- The telephone and fax company
- The post office
- The Banks
- The credit companies

24

Employee

The company must conduct exit interviews with employee(s) and give at least a 2 weeks exit notice.

Employee

The inventory of the agency properties must be done and disbursed in the following ways.

1. Make the list of all items
2. Make donation of items
3. Dispose unusable items

the Author

The author was a director of home healthcare organization. She reviewed policy for State regulations, performed the job of quality assurance and participated in the State survey of home health facilities. She was recognized for excellent performance with promotion, recognition, and cash-award of $1000.00 from home care Council of New York City.

The author received letter of voluntary closure from Georgia department of community Health following the zero violation of the exit survey of home health care services. She was in the Dean's list at St Joseph College of New York for her scholastic achievements; awarded best nurse of the month at Emory University teaching hospital Atlanta Georgia, recognized for Flu Vaccine health fair by community council of great Dallas TX, received her 11 years of service recognition for dedicated services at Woodhull hospital New York, Volunteer services at Washington hospital center and Red cross society Dallas, Texas and many more accolades. Although, the author is retired from healthcare, she has become the author of many books. She has written this book to share her experience of starting new home healthcare and assist whoever wants to start a home healthcare business.

Apart from being a Registered Nurse in the United States with broad experience in different healthcare settings and socio-cultural environments, she was a midwife and Ophthalmic nurse from Nigeria who migrated to United States in the early 1990. Since then, she schooled, worked at different healthcare facilities (i.e mental health, immunizations units of department of health, Clinician in a Medical/ Surgical/Nephrology hospital).

Made in the USA
Columbia, SC
29 June 2023